EARTHQUAKES

By Ian Graham

Publisher: Melissa Fairley
Editor: Miranda Smith
Designer: Emma Randall
Production Controller: Ed Green
Production Manager: Suzy Kelly

ISBN-13: 978-1-84898-105-8 pbk

Picture credits (t=top; b=bottom; c=centre; OFC= outside front cover; OBC=outside back cover)
Diana Bier Torre Mayor/Alamy: 61. Caro/Alamy: 4–5. Courtesy CRASAR, University of South
Florida/ Office of Legislative and Public Affairs: 58t. William Crawford/Integrated Ocean Drilling
Program: 11b. Dan Dzurisin/HVO/USGS: 48–49. FEMA/Department of Homeland Security: 35b.
Geoeye/Science Photo Library: 19t. Peter Ginter/Science Faction/Corbis: 58–59t. David
Hardy/Science Photo Library: 23b. Gary Hincks/Science Photo Library: 7t, 15t, 43t. iStock: 28b,
32, 33r. Benjamin Lowy/Corbis 40b. Pierre Merchal/Look at Sciences/Science Photo Library: 18b.
Carlos Munoz-Yague/ Eurelios/Science Photo Library: 57b. NASA: 37t. NASA/GSFC/LaRC/JPL,
MISR Team: 49t. NASA Human Spaceflight Collection: 44–45b. NASA Johnson Space Center
Collection: 30–31. National Geophysical Data Center/NOAA: 29t, 33t, 36t. NOAA: 42. David
Parker/Science Photo Library: 12, 13t. PhotoDisc: 50–51t all. Bart Pro/Alamy: 32t.
Louie Psihoyos/Science Faction/Corbis: 60b. Reuters/Corbis: OFC. Shutterstock: 1 all, 2,
3A–G, 6l, 7r, 9, 10l, 10–11t, 11r, 11r (background), 14 all, 15r, 15r (background), 16–17 all, 18l,
19r, 19r (background), 20–21 all, 22, 23r, 24–25 all, 26–27 all, 28l, 29r, 30l, 31r, 31r (background),
34l, 35r, 35r (background), 36l, 37r, 37r (background), 38–39 all, 40l, 41 all, 44l, 45r, 45r
(background), 48l, 49r, 49r (background), 50l, 51r, 52l, 53r, 54l, 55r, 55r (background), 58l, 59r,
60l, 61r, 62, 63, 64, OBC all. USGS: 6, 47, 52t, 53b. USGS/NASA: 51b. Michael S.
Yamashita/Corbis: 57t. Sam Yeh/AFP/Getty Images: 54–55. ticktock Media Archive: 8b.

Every effort has been made to trace copyright holders, and we apologize in advance for any
omissions. We would be pleased to insert the appropriate acknowledgments in any subsequent
edition of this publication.

NOTE TO READERS

The website addresses are correct at the time of publishing. However, due to the ever-changing nature
of the internet, websites and content may change. Some websites can contain links that are unsuitable
for children. The publisher is not responsible for changes in content or website addresses. We advise
that internet searches should be supervised by an adult.

CONTENTS

THE EARTH IS A CRACKED EGG!

SEVERAL TIMES A YEAR, THE MEDIA FOCUS ON PART OF THE WORLD WHERE THE GROUND HAS BEEN SHAKEN VIOLENTLY BY AN EARTHQUAKE. SCIENTISTS ALL OVER THE WORLD STUDY THESE DRAMATIC EVENTS AND THEIR CAUSES. THE GROUND UNDER YOUR FEET SEEMS SOLID AND STEADY, BUT SCIENTISTS NOW KNOW IT IS ACTUALLY MOVING.

WHY DOES THE GROUND MOVE?

Until the 1960s, the idea that continents made of solid rock were moving seemed crazy. However, scientists now know that the Earth's **crust** is a thin, rocky shell floating on top of hot rock called the **mantle**. The mantle is solid, but it can flow slowly like thick treacle. And the mantle does move, driven by heat that rises up from deep within the planet. As the mantle moves, it carries the Earth's crust with it.

EGG-SHELL EARTH

The Earth's crust is divided into a series of plates – called **tectonic plates** – just like the cracked shell of a boiled egg. The tectonic plates move in different directions at different speeds. The edges of the plates grind together and the places where they meet are called **faults**. The plates do not slip past each other smoothly. They stick and then slip suddenly. These sudden movements at faults produce earthquakes.

MAKING MAPS OF PLATES

Scientists from the California Institute of Technology and the Scripps Institution of Oceanography are studying how the Antarctic plate at the South Pole fits with all the plates around it. The scientists' work will help other scientists to produce a more accurate map of the Earth's crust.

This beach on Sumatra was devastated by a giant wave following the Indonesian earthquake of 2007.

WHO STUDIES EARTHQUAKES?

A major branch of science is devoted to understanding the Earth, its structure, how it changed in the past and how it is still changing today. It is such a big subject that scientists often specialize. **Geophysicists** are Earth scientists who study the physical properties of the planet, and its seas and atmosphere. **Geologists** study the Earth's rocks. **Geochemists** study the chemistry of rocks. **Geomorphologists** study the Earth's land masses and the processes that shaped them. All of these scientists may also study earthquakes. In addition, there are earthquake engineers, who study the design and construction of buildings, bridges and other structures in places where earthquakes are common. Their job is to reduce the amount of damage that structures suffer when they are shaken by an earthquake.

EARTHQUAKE SCIENTISTS

Scientists who specialize in studying earthquakes are called **seismologists**. A few seismologists specialize in studying ancient earthquakes. These scientists are called **palaeoseismologists**. Seismology is a young science. Until the late 1800s, scientists thought underground explosions caused earthquakes, and the quakes caused faults in the ground.

A US Geological Survey scientist sets up his equipment on the east side of the Mount St Helens volcano in Washington state, USA. The Mount Adams volcano can be seen in the background.

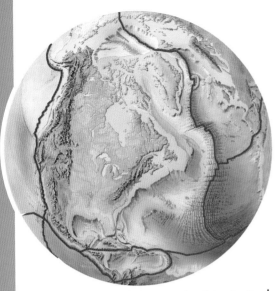

At the boundaries of the tectonic plates (red), sudden movements cause earthquakes.

But after a terrible earthquake in San Francisco in 1906, scientist Harry Fielding Reid had an idea. He thought sudden movements of the faults caused earthquakes, and was later proved correct.

TEAMWORK

Today, scientists who study earthquakes usually work in teams. Scientists and engineers from different universities, sometimes even in different countries, work together to try to understand earthquakes better. They work with computers and use information provided by satellites in space. When not in front of their computers, they are usually studying rocks and faults on field trips anywhere in the world.

A CAREER IN SCIENCE

Dr Lucy Jones is the head of the US Geological Survey office in Pasadena, California. She studied physics, but after spending time in Taiwan, a major earthquake zone, she switched to geology. She has a doctorate in geophysics from the Massachusetts Institute of Technology.

A DAY IN THE LIFE OF ...

Dr Jones works in California, USA, one of the world's most active earthquake regions. Her research includes studying the tremors that occur before and after a big earthquake, and how they might be used to forecast future quakes. When California is rocked by a quake, it is often Dr Jones who explains to the public what has happened. She and her colleagues also advise officials and politicians on the policies needed to make California safer.

THE SCIENTIST SAYS ...

If there were a southern California earthquake of 7.8 in magnitude: "We are going to lose all of our natural gas lines, all of our water lines, many of our power lines, most of our transportation systems. We are going to have a disruption to our infrastructure in a way that is going to take months to recover from."

CHAPTER ONE

ON THE MOVE

THE FORCES THAT CAUSE EARTHQUAKES ARE POWERFUL ENOUGH TO MOVE CONTINENTS. AND THAT IS EXACTLY WHAT THEY DO. THE GROUND BENEATH YOUR FEET IS MOVING RIGHT NOW! YOU DO NOT NOTICE IT, BECAUSE IT MOVES ONLY ABOUT AS FAST AS YOUR FINGERNAILS AND TOENAILS GROW.

CONTINENTAL DRIFT

The discovery that the Atlantic Ocean is growing wider every year helped scientists to understand why earthquakes happen. In the early 1900s, the German scientist Alfred Wegener noticed a similarity in the coasts of South America and Africa. He wondered if these continents might once have fitted together and then drifted apart. This theory of **continental drift** sparked research that unlocked the secrets of earthquakes.

MAPPING THE SEABED

In the 1950s, scientists making maps of the seabed discovered a huge mountain chain snaking around the Earth under the sea. It is called the **mid-ocean ridge**. At 75,000km long, it is the longest mountain chain on Earth, but it is completely hidden underwater!

The mid-ocean ridge marks the boundary between two tectonic plates. The plates either side are moving apart and new crust is created as magma (melted rock) is pushed up.

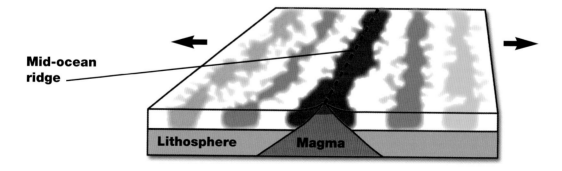

Mid-ocean ridge

Lithosphere   Magma

MAGNETIC SEABED

The seabed is covered with invisible magnetic stripes! Each stripe is tens of kilometres wide and magnetized in the opposite direction to the stripes on each side of it. Scientists finally explained this in the 1960s. **Magma** (liquid rock) wells up through the middle of the mountains and pushes the seabed on each side further apart. When it cools and hardens, its magnetism lines up with the Earth's magnetism. From time to time, the Earth's magnetism reverses. So does the magnetism of new seabed that forms afterwards. Over millions of years, the Earth's magnetism reverses again and again and produces the magnetic stripes. This discovery proved that the ocean floor is spreading wider and carrying the continents on their tectonic plates with it. Until recently, very little was known about the end of the mid-ocean ridge – which is located at Iceland – because it is usually hidden underneath sea-ice. But now, a team of scientists in icebreaking ships have studied this part of the seabed under the Arctic.

This aerial photograph taken of part of the Icelandic coast shows the fault line between the European and North American tectonic plates.

Earthquakes in the Himalayan mountains are caused by the tectonic plate carrying India pushing north into the Asian tectonic plate.

WHERE DID THE CONTINENTS DRIFT FROM?

Millions of years ago, there was one huge supercontinent called Pangaea. Pangaea covered half the Earth, while the rest was covered by an enormous ocean. Then, about 200 million years ago, Pangaea started to break up. First, it split into two parts, Laurasia and Gondwanaland. In time, they broke up to form the continents we have today. Laurasia produced the northern continents and Gondwanaland formed the southern continents. Water flooded into the spaces between them and became the oceans.

MAKING MOUNTAINS

New crust has been forming and spreading out for millions of years. It should have made the Earth bigger, but it did not. When two continents collide, their edges crumple together. Some of the rock is pushed upwards and forms mountains. India, pushing north into Asia, formed the Himalayan mountain chain in this way. The Himalayas have been growing for about 40 million years and they are still growing today. In 1994, researchers placed an instrument near the summit of Mount Everest, the world's highest mountain. It uses radio signals from satellites in space to measure any movement of the mountain. Its readings show that Mount Everest grows about 4mm higher every year.

▶ ▶ http://pubs.usgs.gov/gip/dynamic/historical.html

The ocean floor is made of heavier rock than a continent. When an ocean floor collides with a continent, the heavier ocean plate slides underneath. This 'subduction' takes place in **subduction zones**. And the biggest earthquakes happen at subduction zones. With these discoveries, scientists began to understand the processes that make the continents move and produce earthquakes.

In 1985, the *Joides Resolution* drilling ship (below) replaced the *Glomar Challenger* (see column right).

INVESTIGATING THE EVIDENCE: HOW OLD IS THE OCEAN FLOOR?

The investigation: Scientists wanted to provide evidence of the ongoing spreading of the sea-floor and prove the theory of continental drift.

The scientists: A team of scientists from the US National Science Foundation and the University of California.

Collecting the evidence: If the ocean floor is still being formed and spreading out, then it should be made from much younger rock than the rest of the Earth's crust. A deep-sea research and drilling ship called *Glomar Challenger* was specially designed to research this theory. From August 1968, the ship criss-crossed the mid-Atlantic ridge from South America to Africa, drilling 1,740m into the ocean floor at a depth of 7,000m. The team brought up rock samples to take back to the laboratory for study and analysis.

The conclusion: The team proved that, although the Earth is 4,500 years old, the oldest rocks from the ocean floor are only 200 million years old. The rocks' average age is only 60 million years. This research showed that new ocean floor is forming all the time. It proved that sea-floor spreading and continental drift really happen.

CHAPTER TWO

EARTHQUAKE ALERT!

NEWS PICTURES OF AN EARTHQUAKE USUALLY SHOW THE DAMAGE LEFT BEHIND. BUT IT CAN BE A VERY COMPLICATED STORY. AN EARTHQUAKE OFTEN BEGINS WITH A MILD TREMBLING OF THE GROUND. IT MAY BE SO SLIGHT THAT YOU DO NOT NOTICE, BUT SCIENTIFIC INSTRUMENTS CAN DETECT IT. IT IS THE FIRST HINT THAT ENORMOUS SLABS OF ROCK ARE BEGINNING TO MOVE UNDERGROUND.

This aerial photograph shows the San Andreas fault as it crosses the Carrizo Plain 450km south of San Francisco, in California, USA. The fault extends almost the full length of California.

A teacher in Parkfield's one-room schoolhouse drilled schoolchildren at least once a month in what to do if there was an earthquake. The building is earthquake-resistant, with shatter-proof windows.

FIRST SHOCKS

The first trembles in the ground are called **foreshocks**. Soon afterwards, the ground is rocked by the earthquake's main shock. This may be just strong enough to shake things off tables, or it may be powerful enough to shatter buildings. When the dust settles, the earthquake has not finished. Over the following days or weeks, the ground may shake again. These are known as **aftershocks**. Each foreshock and aftershock is an earthquake in its own right.

THE PARKFIELD EXPERIMENT

The town of Parkfield stands on the San Andreas fault in California, USA. Earthquakes of about **magnitude** 6 happen at Parkfield every 10–30 years. Since the 1980s, dozens of instruments have been dotted around the town to record the tiniest movement of the ground. Then the scientists waited for the next earthquake, which was expected by about 1993. But they had to wait longer than they expected – the earthquake finally struck in 2004.

The primary and secondary waves of an earthquake can act as warnings that a strong shake is on the way, and allow people to escape injury when buildings collapse.

THE GROUND RIPPLES

When a huge earthquake hit central Alaska in 2002, a resident of Porcupine Creek said he had seen the solid ground rippling like water and waves 20cm high rolling along the ground! Reports like this hint at how earthquakes spread through the ground. When an earthquake begins, waves of vibrations – **seismic waves** – travel outwards in all directions. The waves are reflected and bent by different layers of rock, like light bouncing off mirrors and being bent by lenses. Scientists can tell where an earthquake began and how powerful it was by studying these waves.

SPEED OF TRAVEL

The first waves of vibrations to arrive are the **p waves**, or primary waves. P waves are often very small and cause little or no damage. They travel through the ground at an amazing speed of more than 20,000km/h – more than 20 times faster than a jumbo jet! Next come more powerful **s waves**, or secondary waves. These travel at 12,000km/h, just over half the speed of p waves. The last waves are **surface**

Earthquakes cause p waves (red), s waves (yellow) and surface waves (mauve) to radiate outwards.

waves, which can be very powerful and shake the ground the most.

P waves can travel right through the Earth and be detected on the other side of the world. S waves travel through most of the Earth, but cannot pass through the solid **core** at the centre. Surface waves travel only across the surface. By studying the times when the different waves arrive, scientists can work out how far away an earthquake is. If they have information from three detectors in different places, they can pinpoint the exact position of the earthquake. The point where it began underground is called its **focus**, or hypocentre. The point on the Earth's surface directly above the focus is the **epicentre**.

INVESTIGATING THE EVIDENCE: WARNING THAT AN EARTHQUAKE IS COMING!

The investigation: To look at earthquakes worldwide and over time in order to work out how to use an earthquake's earliest vibrations to sound a warning before the main shaking begins.

The scientists: Richard M. Allen of the University of Wisconsin-Madison, USA, and Hiroo Kanamori of the California Institute of Technology's Seismological Laboratory, USA.

Collecting the evidence: The two scientists used recorded and witness information from scores of earthquakes past and present all over the world. They considered seismic readings and other geological evidence to develop earthquake early warning systems. They established that the slower and more damaging s waves fall further and further behind the faster p waves as they spread out through the ground.

The conclusion: The harmless p waves can trigger a warning before the more damaging shaking begins. A few seconds' warning gives people enough time to take cover. The result is the development of a warning system called ElarmS (Earthquake Alarm Systems). This system provides warnings in California and other earthquake-prone zones to reduce damage and deaths.

HOW ARE EARTHQUAKES MEASURED?

A quake that hit L'Aquila, Italy, on 6 April 2009 was described as 6.3 on the **Richter Scale**. The Richter Scale is a way of saying how strong an earthquake is. The bigger the number, the stronger the earthquake. The Richter Scale is named after the American seismologist, Charles Richter (1900–1985). When an earthquake happens, scientists look at information recorded by their instruments and use it to calculate the Richter number. It is a way to represent the total amount of energy released by an earthquake. Quakes of less than 2 on the Richter Scale – also called micro-quakes – are too small to be felt, but they can be picked up by instruments. An earthquake has to get to about 4 on the Richter Scale before things start rattling. Increasing the Richter number by one means an earthquake is 10 times bigger. Damage to buildings begins at about 5 on the Richter scale.

OTHER WAYS OF MEASURING QUAKES

Scientists often measure quakes in a different way. The length of the fault that slips and the distance it slips produce a number called the Moment Magnitude. This works better than the

In 2008, a deadly earthquake measuring 7.9 on the Richter scale hit the Sichuan Province of China, and at least 68,000 people were killed. The earthquake was felt more than 1,700km away, in both Beijing and Shanghai, as well as in neighbouring countries.

Richter Scale for measuring the biggest earthquakes. The Italian scientist Guiseppe Mercalli (1850–1914) drew up a **Mercalli quake scale** that does not need any scientific instruments. Instead, it is based on the damage people see around them, so anyone can use it. It is a 12-point scale. The more damage you see, the bigger the Mercalli number or **intensity**.

GETTING IT RIGHT

Sometimes, scientists have to change the recorded magnitude of an earthquake as they learn more about it. That is what happened when a massive earthquake happened near Sumatra in 2004. As scientists gathered more information about it, they found it was stronger than they had first thought.

A CAREER IN SCIENCE

After taking a degree in physics, Peter Molnar was awarded a doctorate in Geology (Seismology) from Columbia University, USA, in 1970. He is now Professor of Geological Sciences at the University of Colorado, Boulder.

A DAY IN THE LIFE OF …

Dr Molnar's wide-ranging work includes studies of the way the Earth's crust moves and changes shape, especially where mountains are forming in places such as the Himalayan range. In 2001, after studying the earthquake history of the Himalayas, Dr Molnar wrote that major earthquakes in other parts of Asia were overdue, and that the death toll could be very high. On 8 October 2005, a devastating earthquake struck the region. However, geologists' understanding of such earthquakes is still not far enough advanced for them to accurately predict catastrophic events.

THE SCIENTIST SAYS …

"If a slip between the Indian Shield and the Himalayan crystalline nappes occurs largely by slip associated with major earthquakes, then recurrence intervals of such earthquakes are likely to be between 200 and 500 years, with a likely value of 300 years."

WHAT DO QUAKES SOUND LIKE?

Anyone who has experienced an earthquake knows that they are noisy. Windows shatter. Bricks and concrete crash to the ground. Shelves and cupboards shed their contents on the floor. But even without all of these sounds of destruction, the earthquakes themselves make noise.

HOW CAN YOU HEAR A QUAKE?

The human ear is sensitive to vibrations as slow as about 20 per second and as fast as about 20,000 per second. Earthquakes produce vibrations within this range. When the ground shakes, the air above the ground shakes as well and we hear these vibrations in the air as sound. Bigger earthquakes produce big, slow, ground movements, which produce long, low, rumbling sounds. Smaller earthquakes generate small, fast, ground movements, which produce shorter, high-pitched bangs. People who live in places where there are very few big earthquakes often mistake the sound of an earthquake for something else – for example, a clap of thunder or an explosion.

This scientist is looking at a computer readout of seismic activity. This kind of monitoring is often the only way that we find out about silent earthquakes.

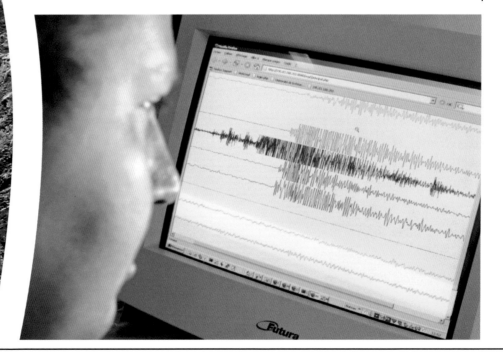

▶▶ http://news.bbc.co.uk/1/hi/in_depth/2059330.stm

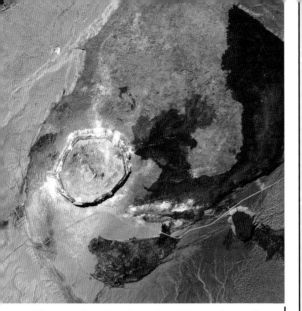

Silent earthquakes have been happening under the Kilauea volcano (here seen from space).

SILENT QUAKES

Scientists used to think that all earthquakes are noisy until they found evidence for silent quakes. The more slowly the ground shakes, the lower the sound it makes. Eventually, it moves so slowly that the human ear cannot hear anything. Most earthquakes last a few seconds or a few minutes at most, but a fault can go on moving slowly during a silent earthquake for a day or two.

It was recently discovered that, between 1998 and 2005, four silent earthquakes in Hawaii had occurred. Paul Segall, one of the scientists who discovered them, said, "We don't know how common silent earthquakes are because, up to now, we haven't had the capability or tools to measure them."

INVESTIGATING THE EVIDENCE: SILENT EARTHQUAKES

The investigation: Scientists wanted to detect evidence for a silent earthquake and investigate its causes.

The scientists: Paul Segall, a professor of Geophysics at Stanford University, UK, and Peter Cervelli, a geophysicist from the US Geological Survey's Hawaiian Volcano Observatory.

Collecting the evidence: Information from **Global Positioning System (GPS)** satellites in space showed that slip equivalent to a magnitude 5.7 earthquake had happened under Hawaii's Kilauea volcano in November 2000. The earthquake lasted about 36 hours, and, as a result, one side of the volcano slid 8.7cm towards the sea. Because the movement was so slow, it was not detected by normal earthquake instruments and noone felt the ground shaking. The scientists have now recognized that similar events happened in September 1998, July 2003 and January 2005.

The conclusion: At first, the scientists thought unusual rainfall caused the earthquake. They now realize that these slow events are associated with swarms of small, regular earthquakes. It seems that the changes in the earth caused by the slow slip trigger the small quakes.

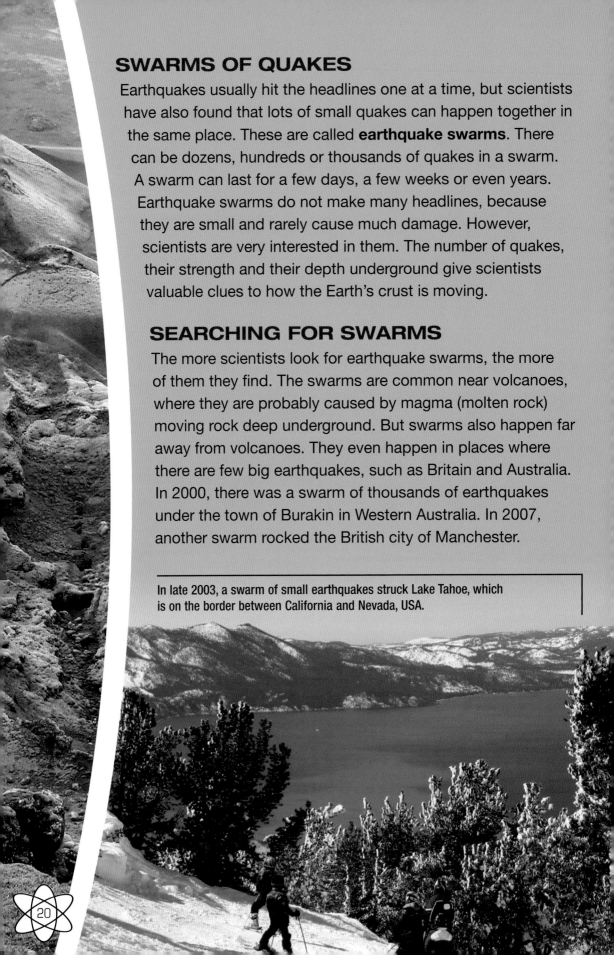

SWARMS OF QUAKES

Earthquakes usually hit the headlines one at a time, but scientists have also found that lots of small quakes can happen together in the same place. These are called **earthquake swarms**. There can be dozens, hundreds or thousands of quakes in a swarm. A swarm can last for a few days, a few weeks or even years. Earthquake swarms do not make many headlines, because they are small and rarely cause much damage. However, scientists are very interested in them. The number of quakes, their strength and their depth underground give scientists valuable clues to how the Earth's crust is moving.

SEARCHING FOR SWARMS

The more scientists look for earthquake swarms, the more of them they find. The swarms are common near volcanoes, where they are probably caused by magma (molten rock) moving rock deep underground. But swarms also happen far away from volcanoes. They even happen in places where there are few big earthquakes, such as Britain and Australia. In 2000, there was a swarm of thousands of earthquakes under the town of Burakin in Western Australia. In 2007, another swarm rocked the British city of Manchester.

In late 2003, a swarm of small earthquakes struck Lake Tahoe, which is on the border between California and Nevada, USA.

In a month, the British Geological Survey recorded six quakes up to 2.4 on the Richter Scale. In 2002, more than 20 quakes were recorded there, reaching 3.9 on the Richter Scale. Swarms also occur in places where big earthquakes are common, such as the USA and Japan.

On 27 February 2005, an earthquake swarm began under the Pacific Ocean off the northwest coast of the USA. In less than six days, 3,742 earthquakes were recorded. At times, there were as many as 70 quakes per hour.

SUPER-SWARMS

Some swarms have so many quakes in such a short time that they are called super-swarms. A super-swarm of more than 7,000 quakes struck the seabed near Tokyo, Japan, over a period of just two months in 2000.

INVESTIGATING THE EVIDENCE: THE MYSTERY OF THE MOVING MOUNTAIN

The investigation: In 2003, Slide Mountain, Nevada, USA, rose nearly 8mm. Scientists investigated a link between this and a swarm of earthquakes below Lake Tahoe.

The scientists: A team of scientists led by Ken Smith from the University of Nevada's Seismological Laboratory, USA, and Geoff Blewitt, a geophysicist with the university's Nevada Bureau of Mines and Geology.

Collecting the evidence: Sensitive instruments on Slide Mountain in Nevada, USA, showed that it suddenly moved upwards and towards the northwest at the end of 2003. The movement of the mountain happened at the same time as a swarm of nearly 1,600 small earthquakes underneath it and the nearby Lake Tahoe.

The conclusion: The movement of Slide Mountain seems to have been caused by magma moving around underground, forcing several kilometres of rock apart, and causing the surface to rise.

CHAPTER THREE

PLATE COLLISION

THE BIG EARTHQUAKES ARE CAUSED BY FAULTS AROUND THE EDGES OF THE EARTH'S GREAT TECTONIC PLATES. BUT EARTHQUAKES ALSO HAPPEN IN OTHER PLACES. ON THE MORNING OF 1 MAY 2005, RESIDENTS OF THE US STATE OF ARKANSAS AWOKE TO FIND THE GROUND SHAKING. THE STATE IS NOT NEAR THE EDGE OF A TECTONIC PLATE, SO WHY DID THE GROUND SHAKE?

Lesser flamingoes flock together in the waters of Lake Nakuru, in the Great Rift Valley of east Africa. The valley is being created by two great tectonic plates pulling apart.

SLOW-MOTION CRASH

The great plates of the Earth's crust can move in three ways to cause earthquakes. The plates can push together, slide against each other or move apart. For example, earthquakes in northern India and Pakistan are caused by two plates colliding with each other like a slow-motion car crash. Earthquakes in California, on the west coast of the USA, are caused by two plates sliding past each another. And earthquakes in east Africa happen because the whole continent is splitting in two and the two plates are moving apart. The land between them is collapsing and forming the Great Rift Valley. Eventually, east Africa will split away from the rest of the continent and the Indian Ocean will rush in to create a new sea.

STRETCHING NORTH AMERICA

The US state of Arkansas is far away from the edge of the crust plate that the USA sits on, yet some of the biggest earthquakes in North America happened there in the early 1800s. And earthquakes are still happening there today. Scientists think that North America tried to rip itself apart hundreds of millions of years ago, but did not quite finish the job. The middle of the continent was stretched, causing cracks called rifts. The ground is still moving today, and this causes up to 200 small quakes a year.

This diagram shows tectonic plates colliding. At the top in the centre is an oceanic tectonic plate. Magma pushed up by the activity of the core and mantle inside the Earth arrives at the surface and spreads out. This forces the outer edges of the oceanic plate under the neighbouring coastal plates.

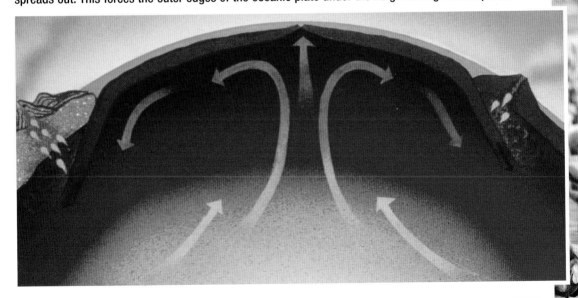

Dams are needed to collect water for people to use, but the weight of the water above a fault in the Earth's surface could be the cause of earthquakes.

WHAT ELSE CAUSES QUAKES?

Anything that alters the balance of forces in the ground can trigger an earthquake. Extra weight pressing on the ground can make a fault slip. When a reservoir is built by flooding a valley, millions of tonnes of water collects at the top. When the reservoir behind the Oroville dam in northern California was filled in 1975, a magnitude 5.7 quake shook the area. It may have been triggered by the extra weight of the water.

THE MOON AND QUAKES

The Moon's gravity pulls the Earth's oceans towards it. A big bulge of water forms on the side of the Earth closest to the Moon. A smaller bulge forms on the opposite side of the Earth. As the Earth spins, these bulges of water move around it. As a bulge passes by, it causes a high tide. The two bulges produce two high tides each day. The seashore is pressed down by a huge extra weight of water with each high tide and this may be enough to trigger a quake in some places. The Earth's crust itself is pulled as the Moon passes overhead

▶▶ http://dsc.discovery.com/news/2009/04/06/earth-tide-quake.html

At 509.2m, the Taipei 101 is the tallest skyscraper in Taiwan and one of the tallest in the world.

and this may also be enough to trigger earthquakes.

CAN SKYSCRAPERS CAUSE QUAKES?

Skyscrapers are amazingly heavy. One of the world's tallest buildings is Taipei 101 in Taiwan, which weighs 700,000 tonnes. Cheng-Horng Lin, a geologist from the National Taiwan Normal University, thinks the great weight of this building, which may rest on an earthquake fault line, could have triggered earthquakes. While it was being built, the number of small earthquakes began to increase. And two larger earthquakes have occurred since it was completed.

INVESTIGATING THE EVIDENCE: TIDES AND EARTHQUAKES

The investigation: To provide evidence that earthquakes can be triggered by Earth's tides, which are produced by the gravitational pull of the Moon and Sun on the Earth.

The scientists: Professor John Vidale and Elizabeth Cochrane from the University of California, Los Angeles, USA.

Collecting the evidence: The team analyzed records of 2,000 earthquakes that were stronger than magnitude 5.5 and that occurred between 1977 and 2000. Seismologists at Harvard University provided the earthquake data. The tide calculations were provided by Sachiko Tanaka of Japan's National Research Institute for Earth Science and Disaster Prevention.

The conclusion: The team provided the evidence that high tides can indeed cause earthquakes. Earth tides cause the oceans' waters to slosh, which in turn raises and lowers stresses on faults in the Earth's surface twice a day. The team found that about three-quarters of the earthquakes they studied happened when tidal forces were at their greatest, and that large tides can have a significant effect. They showed that a rise in sea level of only 2m is enough to trigger an earthquake. It would have happened anyway, but a high tide can make it happen sooner.

CAN QUAKES CAUSE QUAKES?

Every year, all over the world, there are more than 50,000 earthquakes strong enough to be felt. Scientists used to think they were all separate events, and that one earthquake did not cause other earthquakes. But now scientists are beginning to find connections between earthquakes and that one may be triggering others. Some earthquakes seem to be able to cause others some distance away. When a fault slips and causes an earthquake, the forces that made the fault slip do not always disappear. They may move along the fault and trigger another earthquake elsewhere.

UNZIPPING A FAULT

If earthquakes happen one after another along a fault, like a row of dominoes falling over, it is called an **earthquake storm**. Earthquake storms can keep going for a long time. The best known earthquake storm has

been happening in Turkey for the past 70 years. Earthquakes have been erupting and moving westwards along a crack in the ground called the North Anatolian fault since 1939. Now, scientists think the shock waves spreading out from a strong earthquake can also shake a distant fault enough to start it moving. The first clue that this might be happening came in 1992 when a strong earthquake rocked the town of Landers in southern California, USA. It was the strongest quake to hit the area for 40 years. As shock waves spread out through the ground, more earthquakes were recorded throughout the western USA. They started within minutes of the Landers quake and went on for months. Some of them occurred under the Yellowstone National Park in Wyoming, more than 1,200km from Landers.

Geysers at Yellowstone National Park were affected by mini-quakes under the park set off by a distant quake in Alaska.

INVESTIGATING THE EVIDENCE: LONG-DISTANCE EARTHQUAKES

The investigation: In 2002, a powerful earthquake not only rocked Alaska but may also have changed the timing and behaviour of Yellowstone National Park's **geysers**. Scientists set out to find the evidence for this long-distance effect.

The scientists: A team of scientists led by Robert Smith, professor of geology and geophysics at the University of Utah, USA.

Collecting the evidence: The team studied Yellowstone National Park in Wyoming, USA. As the waves of vibrations from the strong earthquake in Alaska in 2002 passed through the Earth, more than 1,000 small earthquakes were detected under the park. Geysers – hot springs where steam and hot water spurt out from time to time – were affected too. Several geysers erupted more often and the temperature of the water in one of the geysers more than doubled.

The conclusion: The Alaskan earthquake had indeed set off small earthquakes more than 3,000km away in Wyoming.

THE BIGGEST EARTHQUAKES

The world's biggest earthquakes make the biggest headlines. They are also called megathrust earthquakes or **mega-quakes**. They happen at places where one of the Earth's crust plates is sliding underneath another plate. The edges of the plates lock together but the plates keep moving. The crust bends, little by little, perhaps for hundreds or thousands of years. Then, all the energy stored up in the fault is suddenly released in a shattering mega-quake. Mega-quakes last longer than other earthquakes.

A small earthquake, up to about magnitude 5, may last for a few seconds. A bigger, magnitude 8 quake may last up to 60 seconds. But a mega-quake can carry on shaking with enormous force for several minutes.

MEGA-FAULT

One of these mega-quake faults runs for 1,000km along the coast of the northwest USA. When it slips, it will produce a mega-quake. But when will that be? Geologists have studied the evidence in the ground. It shows that this fault produces a really big earthquake every 550 years or so. The last one was 300 years ago.

By analyzing readings on **seismographs** in recording stations, and looking at other evidence, geologists are able to work out what kind of earthquake has occurred.

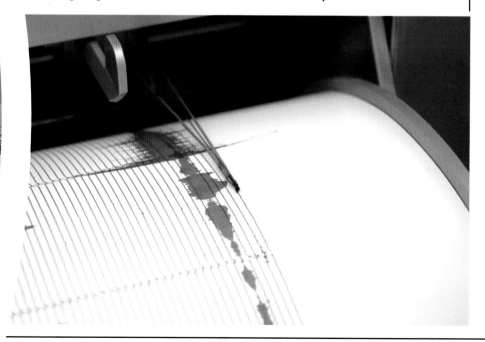

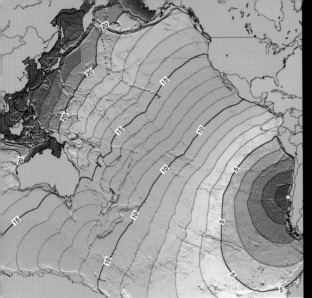

In 1960, there was a mega-quake in Chile, South America that spread right across the Pacific Ocean.

MEGA RECORD

The five most powerful earthquakes since the year 1900 have all been this type of mega-quake. The strongest earthquake ever recorded was a magnitude 9.5 mega-quake that struck Chile in South America on 22 May 1960. But there were even stronger quakes before records began. Seismic waves from the Chilean mega-quake travelled all the way round the world and shook the entire Earth for several days.

DATING MEGA-QUAKES

Scientists would like to know how often mega-quakes have happened in the past. It could give valuable clues to when they might happen again in the future. Sudden changes in ground level can help to date these catastrophic events.

A CAREER IN SCIENCE

Dr Brian Atwater is a geologist who works for the US Geological Survey. He is research professor at the University of Washington. He specializes in the study of large earthquakes and tsunamis in the Pacific Northwest area of the USA.

A DAY IN THE LIFE OF ...

The northwest coast of the USA has been rising steadily for millions of years, because it is being squeezed by the surrounding tectonic plates. Dr Atwater and his team have found an ancient forest of red cedar trees that appeared to have died suddenly when the coast level dropped. This would have flooded the land with seawater, poisoning the cedars. A sudden drop of several metres like this could only have been caused by a catastrophic mega-quake event. By studying the patterns of growth rings in the tree trunks, they established that the trees all died in the same season of the same year. This has provided the first evidence that a mega-quake took place in about the year 1700.

THE SCIENTIST SAYS ...

"Until now, scientists knew about the quake only from geological inference...." But with these studies, the link with the tsunami records is "so strong that those village records become written proof that the earthquake happened."

DO OTHER WORLDS QUAKE?

Scientists have sent space probes to study most of the planets and many of their moons. And they have landed quake detectors on the Moon and Mars. Between 1969 and 1972, Apollo astronauts laid out scientific instruments on the Moon's surface, and the instruments carried on working long after the astronauts returned to Earth. In nearly eight years, instruments on the Moon recorded 12,558 seismic events. Some of these were caused by meteorites (space rocks) crashing into the surface. Others were caused by **moonquakes**.

WHAT CAUSES MOONQUAKES?

Moonquakes are different from earthquakes. The Earth's crust is made of separate crust plates floating on top of the hot mantle. But the Moon cooled down about 3 billion years ago, so it does not have moving crust plates. Some moonquakes happen at the Moon's surface just as the Sun rises. They are caused by sunshine suddenly heating the surface, making it expand and shudder. Most moonquakes start hundreds of kilometres underground. As the Moon circles the Earth and the Earth circles the Sun, the Moon is pulled and squashed by their gravity. These forces are powerful enough to cause quakes.

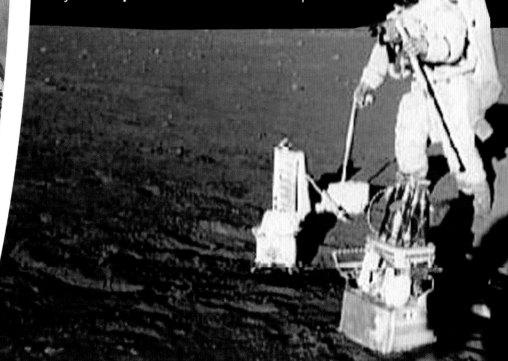

ARE THERE QUAKES ON MARS?

When the Viking 2 spacecraft landed on Mars in 1976, it carried an instrument that recorded a **marsquake**. Spacecraft have been photographing Mars for decades, so scientists are able to compare photographs taken years apart. Some of these 'before and after' photographs show changes that may have been caused by quakes. Boulders have fallen down slopes and there is evidence of landslides.

SUNQUAKES

Surprisingly, even our star, the Sun, experiences quakes. The Sun has no solid surface, but enormous explosions called flares send shock waves rippling across its surface. One flare can explode with as much energy as tens of thousands of quakes on Earth.

Alan Bean sets up the Apollo Lunar Surface Experimental Package on the Moon's surface during the Apollo 12 mission in 1969.

INVESTIGATING THE EVIDENCE: LOOKING INSIDE THE MOON

The investigation: Scientists at the National Aeronautics and Space Administration (NASA) in the USA wanted to find out what the inside of the Moon is like. To do this they deliberately caused moonquakes.

The scientists: NASA scientists and astronauts.

Collecting the evidence: Rockets and spacecraft that were not needed any more were deliberately crashed into the Moon in the 1970s to cause moonquakes. The vibrations spread through the Moon and these vibrations were picked up by the instruments that had been left on the surface by the Apollo astronauts. The Moon rang like a bell for up to an hour each time a crash was engineered.

The conclusion: When measurements made by the Apollo instruments were studied, they proved for the first time that the Moon has a crust, a mantle and a core.

CHAPTER FOUR

EARTHQUAKE DESTRUCTION

A BIG EARTHQUAKE CAN BE AS POWERFUL AS THOUSANDS OF ATOM BOMBS, SO IT IS NOT SURPRISING THAT EARTHQUAKES CAUSE TERRIBLE DESTRUCTION. BUT BIG EARTHQUAKES CAN DO A LOT MORE THAN KNOCK DOWN HOUSES. THEY CAN CHANGE THE SHAPE OF A COAST OR EVEN MOVE WHOLE ISLANDS. WHEN EARTHQUAKES HIT THE HEADLINES, THE REPORTS OFTEN INCLUDE NEWS OF THE DEATHS AND INJURIES THEY CAUSED. MOST LIVES ARE NOT LOST BECAUSE OF THE EARTHQUAKE ITSELF, BUT BY BUILDINGS COLLAPSING.

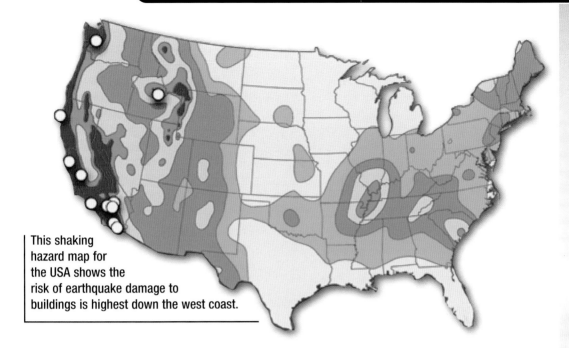

This shaking hazard map for the USA shows the risk of earthquake damage to buildings is highest down the west coast.

VULNERABLE VICTIMS

When the Landers earthquake struck California in 1992, 750 people were left homeless. When an earthquake of similar strength struck Pakistan in 2005, it left 3 million people homeless. Houses in poorer countries suffer so much more damage because of the way they are built and the materials that they are made of. They are often built from mud bricks, and when an earthquake shakes them, they crumble and collapse completely. Because of this, earthquakes in poorer countries often cause much greater numbers of deaths and injuries. Only one person was killed by the Landers earthquake, while the Pakistan earthquake killed nearly 75,000 people.

MAPPING DANGERS

Earthquake scientists draw up maps called 'shaking-hazard maps'. They show where the danger from earthquake shaking is the highest. Officials use them to draw up rules and regulations for constructing safer buildings in those areas. Scientists and engineers study how buildings are damaged by shaking model buildings, using platforms called **shake tables**. The tables can be programmed to shake in exactly the same way as a real earthquake.

In the USA, nearly 75 per cent of Utah's population lives near the Wasatch Fault. Movement on this fault has lifted the Wasatch Range to form a spectacular background immediately behind Salt Lake City.

Iceland's Lake Kleifarvatn sprang a leak after an earthquake tore open the ground in 2000. The waters dropped more than 4m the following year, leaving a barren lake bed.

CHANGING LANDSCAPE

Damaged buildings and roads can be repaired, but earthquakes can also make more permanent changes to the landscape itself. If loose earth and rock on a hillside are shaken free, gravity does the rest. A whole hillside can slide down into a valley. Houses built near the edge of a cliff or on a hillside are in danger of collapsing as the ground underneath slips away. A small landslide may block a road, but a large one can bury a whole village. Some landslides are big enough to be seen from space.

COASTAL CHANGE

The coastline of New Zealand was changed by a strong earthquake in 1931. At Napier on the North Island, a line of cliffs stands a couple of kilometres inland from the seashore – they used to be at the water's edge. The 1931 earthquake lifted the coast and left it 2m higher than before. The seabed under the cliffs became the new seashore. Future earthquakes will push the coast up even higher. Earthquakes can move whole islands as well. A series of earthquakes under the sea off Japan in 2000 moved the islands of Niijima and Kozujima nearly 1m further apart. An earthquake in 2004 moved Sumatra several metres closer to Indonesia.

PULLING THE PLUG

Earthquakes are powerful enough to open up cracks in the ground. If the ground cracks open near a lake or river, water may drain away into it, like pulling the plug in a bath. Lake Kleifarvatn in Iceland is draining into a new crack that was probably opened by an earthquake.

An earthquake can shake a whole hillside free, carrying houses with it.

INVESTIGATING THE EVIDENCE: DISAPPEARING LAKE

The investigation: In 2000, an earthquake opened a fissure in Lake Kleifarvatn in Iceland. Scientists want to find out why and how quickly the lake is disappearing. The lake was 6km long and 2.3km wide. In only a year, it shrank to 3.5km long and 1.8km wide.

The scientists: Geologist Amy Clifton and her colleagues at the Nordic Volcanological Institute in Reykjavik, Iceland.

Collecting the evidence: The team found a gash in the ground 30cm wide and 400m long at the lake's edge. The scientists found that they could actually hear the water draining away by putting an ear to the ground! The team took measurements at the lake and these showed that the water is draining away at the rate of about a centimetre a day.

The conclusion: No earthquake in the Icelandic records has been powerful enough to explain the huge tear in the landscape. The team have proposed that a silent earthquake in 2000 may have caused it. The water may have lubricated the fault lines, allowing them to slide quietly and slowly, avoiding shock waves. The lake will probably not disappear altogether, because the water will find a new, lower level.

Buildings in Niigata, Japan, leaned over because the ground turned to quicksand during an earthquake in 1964.

SINKING BUILDINGS!

When Niigata, in Japan, suffered an earthquake in 1964, photographs of the area showed buildings leaning over at crazy angles. Television pictures of an earthquake in Loma Prieta, California, USA, 25 years later showed buildings leaning in the same way. Some had even sunk into the ground. Experiments flown on the Space Shuttle are helping scientists to understand why.

When wet, sandy soil is shaken by an earthquake, it can flow like a liquid. This effect is called **liquefaction**.

Anything built on top may sink into the ground as if it has changed to quicksand. Whole buildings can sink into 'solid' ground when liquefaction happens. If they sink more on one side than the other, they lean over like the buildings in the Niigata and Loma Prieta earthquakes.

THE SECRETS OF SOIL STRENGTH

Sandy soil depends on the friction between the sand grains for its strength. Normally, the grains of sand lock together. When this kind of soil is shaken by an earthquake, the grains of sand bounce apart and water can get between them. The water lets the sand grains slide past each other

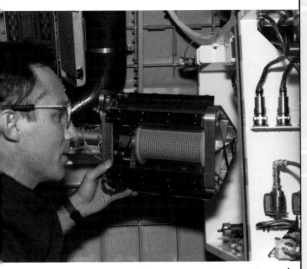

This space shuttle mission astronaut is working on the soil liquefaction experiment.

more easily. As a result, the soil loses its strength and buildings on top may start to sink. As the soil collapses, fountains of water may fly up out of the ground.

SOIL SCIENCE IN SPACE

When scientists tried to study soil liquefaction in their laboratories, gravity pulling on the soil particles distorted the results. It was hard to see which effects were due to gravity and which were due to the soil itself. Scientists wanted to remove the effect of gravity to see what the soil was doing, so they took their experiments into space. Soil liquefaction experiments were flown on-board the Space Shuttle. In space, soil particles are weightless.

INVESTIGATING THE EVIDENCE: TESTING SOIL LIQUEFACTION IN SPACE

The investigation: The aim was to study soil behaviour that could not be duplicated on Earth, finding out about soil liquefaction in the weightless conditions created as the Shuttle orbited the Earth.

The scientists: Buddy Guynes, the experiment's project manager at NASA's Marshall Space Flight Center and his team.

Collecting the evidence: Plastic tubes containing 1.3kg of Ottawa sand were flown on three Space Shuttle missions. In space, they were soaked with water and squashed between two tungsten metal plates. Video cameras recorded what happened. Back on Earth, the samples were X-rayed to reveal how the sand grains had moved.

The conclusion: The experiments revealed new information about the way soil particles lock together that will enable engineers to design stronger foundations for buildings in areas where earthquakes are common.

CAN ANIMALS SENSE EARTHQUAKES?

People interviewed after earthquakes often say that their pets or farm animals behaved strangely just before the earthquake began. The belief that animals can sense earthquakes before people dates back more than 2,000 years, but scientific evidence has been hard to find. The US Geological Survey investigated the effect of earthquakes on animals in the 1970s, but failed to find strong evidence. If an animal's behaviour changes before an earthquake, this does not necessarily mean that the two are connected. There must be many times when animals behave oddly, but if no earthquake follows, their odd behaviour is soon forgotten.

CAN ELEPHANTS HEAR QUAKES COMING?

If animals really can sense earthquakes, how might they be doing it? Small tremors called foreshocks often occur before an earthquake and many animals are able to sense small vibrations. Elephants are known to communicate using sound so low in pitch that we cannot hear it. This is called infra-sound. Earthquakes produce similar

Elephants may be able to sense an earthquake long before the ground shakes enough for people to notice.

sounds, so animals such as elephants may be able to hear or feel the first rumblings of an earthquake.

ELECTRICITY AND MAGNETISM

Electric and magnetic fields have sometimes been detected at the time of an earthquake. Some birds are known to navigate long distances by sensing the Earth's magnetic field. They may be able to sense these natural magnetic changes. These are all ways that animals might detect earthquakes before people. Small movements in the ground that we cannot feel may release vapours from the soil that animals can detect. Dogs are well-known to have a very sensitive sense of smell.

It is possible that dogs may be able to detect an earthquake through their sense of smell.

INVESTIGATING THE EVIDENCE: ANIMALS AND EARTHQUAKES

The investigation: Just before an earthquake hit the Japanese city of Kobe in 1995, Professor Takeshi Yagi noticed that mice in his laboratory were behaving oddly. He set about designing an experiment to test if the earthquake had caused their strange behaviour, and to provide evidence of animals' ability to sense earthquakes before people.

The scientists: Professor Takeshi Yagi of Osaka University, Japan and his team.

Collecting the evidence: The mice were kept for two weeks in a stable environment so their day–night rhythms could be monitored. They were then exposed to very weak electromagnetic pulses, similar to the electric and magnetic fields detected during earthquakes.

The conclusion: The mice rested less often after exposure to the electromagnetic pulses. All animals, including humans, have an internal clock that regulates their sleep patterns. A mouse's internal clock may be more easily upset by electric and magnetic energy emitted in the days before an earthquake begins. More research is needed.

AFFECTING THE WHOLE EARTH

Earthquakes move enormous amounts of rock. They can shift islands, change coastlines and make huge tracts of land rise or sink. These facts led some scientists to wonder if earthquakes could affect the whole planet. NASA scientists have calculated that the Sumatra earthquake in 2004 was so powerful that it changed the Earth's rotation, shortened the length of a day, changed the planet's shape and shifted the position of the North Pole. It was one of the most powerful earthquakes ever recorded, but even this monster earthquake produced changes that are too small for most people to notice in their everyday lives.

SHORTER DAYS

An earthquake makes the Earth spin a little faster for the same reason that ice skaters spin faster when they pull in their outstretched arms. When an earthquake brings millions of tonnes of rock closer to the Earth's centre, the whole planet spins faster. When the Earth spins faster, the length of each day is shortened. The change is too small to be measured, even with a very accurate stopwatch.

THE EARTH'S SHAPE

The Earth is fatter around the equator than it is around the

Many places, including Bandah Aceh, were completely destroyed by the massive Sumatran earthquake in 2004.

poles. It bulges in the middle because it spins. The Earth's crust tries to fly away from the spinning planet for the same reason that marbles fly off a spinning plate. The spinning motion flings the crust outwards. The equator is affected the most, so the equator bulges and the poles are flattened. The movement of the Earth's crust by the Sumatra earthquake made the Earth a little slimmer around the middle.

MOVING THE POLES

Earthquakes can make the Earth's poles move to new positions. Earthquakes are caused by sudden movements of the Earth's crust, so when the crust moves, this movement changes the balance of the planet. The poles move to bring the Earth back into balance.

Earthquakes can change the shape of the Earth and the way that it spins.

A CAREER IN SCIENCE

Dr William Hammond took a degree in mathematics at the University of California, Berkeley, USA. He was then awarded a doctorate in geological sciences by the University of Oregon. He is now a research professor at the Nevada Bureau of Mines and Geology/ Seismological Laboratory, at the University of Nevada, Reno.

A DAY IN THE LIFE OF ...

Dr Hammond measures movements in the Earth's crust on the western side of the USA. The pattern of these changes helps to explain how the tectonic plates at these sites are moving against each other. His work involves making field trips with teams of scientists to collect data. He has found that seismic activity can cause the Earth's crust and mantle to deform and then relax slowly. This deformation can be detected decades after the original event.

THE SCIENTIST SAYS ...

"We have established 9 new GPS sites around the Tahoe region that can eventually help constrain the depth, location and motion of deep motions of fluids similar to those that have already been observed, and also eventually provide much needed observations ... of the Basin and Range."

CHAPTER FIVE

EARTHQUAKES AND TSUNAMIS

NOT ALL EARTHQUAKES HAPPEN ON LAND. THE EARTH'S CRUST AND THE FAULTS BETWEEN ITS TECTONIC PLATES CONTINUE UNDER THE SEA, SO EARTHQUAKES CAN HAPPEN THERE AS WELL. IF THEY LIFT THE SEABED, THEY CAN CREATE GIANT WAVES CALLED **TSUNAMIS**. ON 26 DECEMBER 2004, AN EARTHQUAKE UNDERNEATH THE INDIAN OCEAN PRODUCED GIANT WAVES THAT SPREAD OUT ACROSS THE OCEAN AND SWEPT ACROSS COASTAL REGIONS CAUSING GREAT DEVASTATION.

The tsunami warning system has a floating surface buoy attached to an anchored seafloor bottom pressure recorder (BPR).

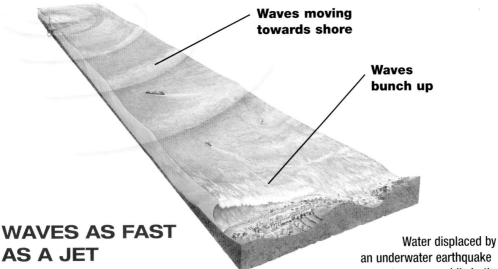

**Waves moving
towards shore**

**Waves
bunch up**

WAVES AS FAST AS A JET

Waves caused by earthquakes are not ordinary waves. If the seabed jumps upwards, it lifts the sea above it as well. The bulge of water flows away in all directions. These waves move amazingly fast – they travel as quickly as a jet airliner! While they are still far out at sea, they may be just a few centimetres high. By the time they reach shallow water near land, they have grown. They grow because the front of the wave slows down and the rest of the wave piles up on top of it. These earthquake waves are called tsunamis. They often reach a height of 15m or so. That is more than seven times the height of a tall adult. But the biggest tsunamis are more than 30m high. Waves as big as this cause great destruction as they sweep across the land.

Water displaced by an underwater earthquake causes waves to move rapidly in the open sea, passing harmlessly under boats (centre). As they approach the shore, the waves slow down and bunch up. A large mass of water crashes ashore as a tsunami, causing destruction.

DETECTING TSUNAMIS

Floating buoys sense movements of the ocean's surface and give an early warning that a tsunami may be on the way. One part of a tsunami detector sits on the seabed and measures the water pressure. The deeper the water is, the more powerfully it will try to crush something. As a tsunami wave rolls over a tsunami detector, the water becomes deeper and the detector measures the rising pressure. It sends the information to a floating buoy, which transmits a message to a warning station.

THE INDIAN OCEAN TSUNAMI

The earthquake that caused the Indian Ocean tsunami of 2004 happened where one of the Earth's tectonic plates is sliding beneath another. The Indian/Australian plate is pushing underneath the Eurasian plate at the rate of 60mm every year. The edge of the Eurasian plate gets dragged down until it cannot bend any more and springs back up, causing an earthquake.

MEGA-FAULT

The fault between the two plates curves around the rim of the Indian Ocean for 5,500km. It passes close to the islands of Sumatra and Java, then heads towards Australia. A long fault like this does not slip all at once. It slips a bit at a time. Many years may pass between these slips and the earthquakes they produce. For example, there were earthquakes at different places on this particular fault in 1833, 1861, 1881, 1935, 2000 and 2002.

JUMPING PLATES

On 26 December 2004, part of the fault near Sumatra slipped. The edge of the Eurasian plate, with Sumatra sitting on top of it, jumped several metres to the west and also jumped upwards by as much as 3m. This lifted the sea

On 26 December 2004, the town of Lhoknga, on the northwest coast of Sumatra, was destroyed when a giant tsunami devastated it and stripped the area of vegetation.

lying above the plate, triggering huge waves. These hit the island of Sumatra first, because it was closest. They swept right across the northern tip of the island, destroying everything in their path. Waves heading in the opposite direction crossed the Indian Ocean and hit the island of Sri Lanka 1,600km away.

STUDYING EVIDENCE

A few months after the earthquake, the US National Science Foundation studied the evidence. They found that this had been an even bigger earthquake than was thought at first. In fact, it set two new earthquake records. It was the greatest length of fault to slip in modern times (about 1,300km) and it went on slipping for the longest time ever recorded (at least 10 minutes).

INVESTIGATING THE EVIDENCE: EARTHQUAKES IN THE FUTURE

The investigation: Following the devastating Indian Ocean earthquake, one of the questions preoccupying everyone is what is the risk of more of these earthquakes?

The scientists: A team led by Professor John McCloskey at the University of Ulster, Northern Ireland, together with a team led by Professor Kerry Sieh at the California Institute of Technology, in the USA.

Collecting the evidence: It is known that large earthquakes change the stress state on nearby geological faults. The teams used satellite photographs, historical records of past earthquakes and computer modelling to work out whether the likelihood of events is increased and to calculate where future earthquakes may occur.

The conclusion: Parts of the faults running through Sumatra and along its coast have not slipped for more than 200 years. The team concluded that the area was at high risk of another earthquake. The faults will undoubtedly give way and cause further large earthquakes and tsunamis, probably in the near future, but no-one knows when.

DETECTING EARTHQUAKES

HOW IS IT POSSIBLE FOR SCIENTISTS TO STUDY AN EARTHQUAKE WHEN THEY DO NOT KNOW WHEN OR WHERE THE NEXT ONE WILL HAPPEN? LUCKILY, EARTHQUAKES CAN BE MEASURED AT A DISTANCE. THE INSTRUMENTS USED TO DETECT AND MEASURE THEM CAN RECORD AN EARTHQUAKE HAPPENING EVEN IF IT IS ON THE OTHER SIDE OF THE WORLD.

DRAGONS KNOW

The first instrument designed to detect earthquakes was invented in China nearly 2,000 years ago. It was a vase with eight dragons' heads around the top. There was a ball in each dragon's mouth and an open-mouthed toad sitting underneath each head. If a quake shook the vase, a ball would drop into a toad's mouth. The ball that fell showed the direction of the quake.

DETECTING EARTHQUAKES TODAY

Dragons' head vases are not used to detect earthquakes any more. Today, earthquakes are measured by instruments called **seismometers**. The first seismometers were made

of a sturdy frame with a pendulum inside. The frame was fixed to the ground. When the ground moved, the frame moved with it, but the pendulum itself stayed still. The movement of the frame compared to the pendulum was recorded by a pen on paper. Modern seismometers use electronic sensors instead of pendulums. They produce digital measurements that can be fed straight into a computer.

TAKING THE EARTH'S PULSE

Scientists use a variety of other instruments to study what happens to the ground during an earthquake. Creepmeters detect very slow movements of the ground.

Strainmeters record changes in the shape of the ground. Tiltmeters measure how much the ground tilts. Magnetometers measure changes in magnetism. The most accurate measurements are made closest to an earthquake, so lots of instruments are dotted around faults where quakes are common.

Invented by Chang Heng in 132 BCE, this Chinese earthquake detector was so sensitive that it detected an earthquake more than 600km away.

SPIES IN SPACE

Earthquakes near big cities make big headlines, but earthquakes in remote parts of the world are equally interesting to scientists. Their remoteness make these earthquakes difficult to study, so scientists often use satellites in space. Many of the satellites in orbit around the Earth study the world's oceans, weather, forests and crops. Luckily, some of them can also detect the effects of earthquakes.

STEERING BY SATELLITE

The Global Positioning System (GPS) is a group of satellites circling the Earth. GPS receivers use radio signals from the satellites to work out their exact position. Ships and airliners use GPS to steer an accurate course. Some cars and trucks have GPS to tell drivers which way to go. And GPS is accurate enough to spot ground movements caused by earthquakes.

THE TERRA SATELLITE

Other satellites are used for earthquake research as well. In 2001, scientists used NASA's Terra satellite to study the effects of a serious earthquake in northern India. Terra was not designed for this. Its mission is to collect information on the effects of human activities on the Earth and its climate. But one of its

This scientist is placing a series of GPS receivers firmly on the ground, If the ground moves, the GPS receivers move too.

http://electronics.howstuffworks.com/gps.htm

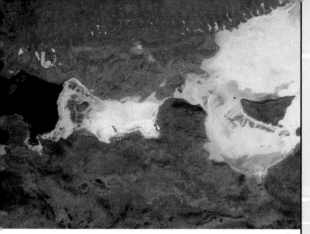

This Terra image was made after the earthquake in India (see right). The image shows areas where groundwater flowed up to the surface.

instruments is also able to see the effects of earthquakes. It uses cameras to look at the colours of light and infrared (heat) rays reflected by the Earth's surface. After the ground is shaken up by a strong earthquake, it reflects light differently. The changes can be seen in pictures taken by Terra.

INVESTIGATING THE EVIDENCE: STUDYING EARTHQUAKES FROM SPACE

The investigation: Researchers wanted to show that satellites can be used to investigate earthquakes in remote parts of the world, in areas that are inaccessible because of devastation or difficult terrain, or in cases where a region is politically sensitive.

The scientists: Bernard Pinty of the Institute for Environment and Sustainability in the joint Research Centre of the European Commission, David J. Diner of NASA's Jet Propulsion Laboratory and colleagues from Germany, France and the USA.

Collecting the evidence: Photographs taken by the Multi-angle Imaging SpectroRadiometer (MISR) instrument on NASA's Terra satellite of northern India before an earthquake struck the region were compared to photographs taken after the earthquake.

The conclusion: The photographs taken by Terra showed water that had been forced out of the soil by the earthquake. A year later, scientists could still see these effects. The water was very salty and the satellite could detect the salt left behind on the ground even after the water had evaporated. Terra showed that satellites are useful for looking at large areas of ground affected by an earthquake.

The three most common types of geological faults are: normal fault (left), thrust fault (centre) and strike-slip fault (right).

FINDING FAULTS

An earthquake at Bam in Iran in 2003 made news for two reasons. First, it was a serious quake that destroyed the town and killed about 30,000 people. Second, it made news among earthquake scientists because it was caused by a fault that noone knew about. Scientists draw maps of the faults in places where earthquakes are common. If they can understand where the faults are, what kind of faults they are, what shape they are and how big they are, the scientists may be able to say where the next big quake is likely to strike. Faults are often easy to spot. Some of them show up as cracks in the ground. Others cause abrupt changes in ground level where one block of ground has been pushed up higher than the next block. But many other faults do not stretch all the way up to the surface. These are known as blind faults.

MAPPING FAULTS UNDER TOKYO

Knowing the depth of faults is vital for estimating the strength of future earthquakes. Scientists can make maps of faults, including blind faults, by setting off explosions in the ground and recording all the reflections of sound waves that bounce off underground layers of rock. When scientists did this in Tokyo, Japan, in 2005, they found that a fault they thought was between 20 and 40km deep is actually as little as 4km under the city.

SCRAPING THE LAND CLEAN

Making a map of faults can be difficult on land when there is a dense covering of plants, because the trees and bushes hide the faults. Scientists in the USA (see right) have found a way of looking through all the thick vegetation with lasers in a process called lidar to make an amazingly accurate map of the ground underneath.

This lidar image was made of Mount St Helens after the volcano erupted.

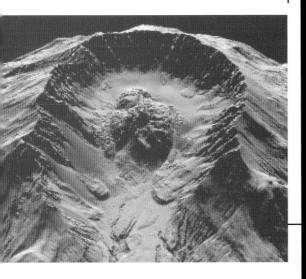

A CAREER IN SCIENCE

Geologist Ralph Haugerud works for the US Geological Survey at the University of Washington Department of Earth and Space, USA. He specializes in surface mapping with a new aerial technology called lidar (light detection and ranging).

A DAY IN THE LIFE OF ...

With colleagues from the US Geological Survey, Ralph Haugerud flies over the ground firing millions of bursts of intense light from lasers at it. The laser beams do not penetrate the vegetation, but a computer is able to process all the reflections that bounce back. It gets rid of reflections from the plants and uses the rest to produce a map of the ground under the vegetation. The scientists have found that using lidar is as if all the vegetation has been scraped off the ground. The work has revealed nearly a dozen faults near Seattle that were not known about before.

THE SCIENTIST SAYS ...

"It's a cumbersome and complex system .... We have to throw away two-thirds of the points .... [But] it provides an amazingly precise view of land surface that cannot be obtained otherwise."

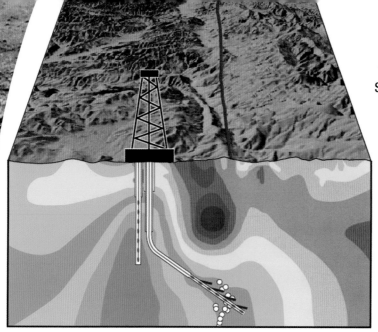

This cross-section of the San Andreas fault zone at Parkfield in California, USA, shows the pilot borehole drilled in 2002 to monitor movement along the fault.

LOOKING BENEATH THE GROUND

News pictures can only show the effects of an earthquake on the surface of the ground, but scientists would like to look under the ground where earthquakes begin. One way to do this is to drill holes called **boreholes** in the ground so that scientists can place their instruments under the surface. The rock that is brought up out of the hole shows the different layers. Water is also brought up out of the borehole to find out how much there is and which chemicals are dissolved in it. The water inside rock and between layers of rock can act like oil in a machine and make the rock more slippery. Then instruments and cameras are lowered down into the hole to take measurements. Sometimes, scientists do not wait for an earthquake to shake up their instruments. They make the ground vibrate by thumping it hard or setting off small explosions. Instruments deep underground in boreholes pick up the vibrations. When the results are studied, they reveal exactly how shaky the ground is.

DRILLING INTO SEATTLE

The city of Seattle in the USA has been shaken by three strong earthquakes in the last 50 years. In 2002, the US Geological Survey drilled two boreholes 150m down into the ground. They revealed the layers of rock underneath the city. Seattle stands on soft sandy rock filling a shallow bowl in the solid **bedrock**. The findings from the boreholes and other tests show that the ground under Seattle seems to behave like a magnifying lens. It strengthens earthquakes and makes the ground shake more violently.

SCRATCHING THE SURFACE

The world's deepest boreholes are about 12km deep. This sounds a lot, but the centre of the Earth is about 3,180km below your feet, so boreholes barely scratch the surface of the planet.

Engineers begin to drill a borehole into the San Andreas fault in California, USA.

INVESTIGATING THE EVIDENCE: DRILLING HOLES IN FAULTS

The investigation: In 2002, at the town of Parkfield in central California, scientists launched a major earthquake drilling project along the San Andreas fault. They wanted to take measurements deep underground inside an active earthquake fault to see what they could learn.

The scientists: Geologists Steve Hickman and William Ellsworth along with colleagues from the US Geological Survey and the US National Science Foundation.

Collecting the evidence: In central California, the San Andreas fault is slipping all the time because of a combination of steady movement and small-magnitude earthquakes. Parkfield, located at the southern end of this, was ideally placed for research. A hole was drilled 3,070m down into the fault near Parkfield and fitted with instruments.

The conclusion: One of the first discoveries is that **tremors** (shakes) coming from more than 30km underground happen a few weeks or months before an earthquake. Scientists will continue to analyze information from the borehole for years to come. It is now called the San Andreas Fault Observatory at Depth, or SAFOD.

PREVENTING EARTHQUAKES

Scientists have made the surprising discovery that ocean storms could be helping to prevent powerful earthquakes – at least on the island of Taiwan. Typhoons are major storms in the western Pacific Ocean that often strike Taiwan during the second half of the year. The scientists believe that these typhoons are triggering slow earthquakes. This type of earthquake has been discovered only recently. Slow earthquakes release their energy over a period of hours or even days, while ordinary, fast earthquakes can occur suddenly and be extremely destructive. People cannot feel slow earthquakes on the ground and instruments such as seismometers cannot measure them, but it is believed that slow earthquakes could help to release pressure and possibly prevent more powerful quakes. Although scientists are still trying to understand how they work, it is possible that they may help to show how and why different kinds of earthquakes take place. This in turn could lead to better earthquake prediction.

UNDER PRESSURE

Although two tectonic plates meet under Taiwan, major earthquakes are rare. Dr Alan Linde and Dr Selwyn Sacks are geophysicists of the Carnegie Institution, Department of Terrestrial

Magnetism. Dr Linde observed: "It's surprising that this area of the globe has had relatively few large earthquakes." Dr Sacks added: "Typhoons reduce the atmospheric pressure on land, but do not affect conditions at the ocean bottom, because water moves into the area and equalizes the pressure."

Regular earthquakes happen after continuous stress along a fault. But when a typhoon reduces atmospheric pressure on land where plates meet, one side of the fault area lifts, releasing the pressure that has been building up inside and triggering a slow earthquake. Dr Linde thinks it is sensible to assume that these slow earthquakes may reduce the frequency of larger and more damaging earthquakes.

A giant wave hits the shore near a fishing harbour in eastern Taiwan in 2007 during Typhoon Krosa, which pounded the coast with powerful winds and torrential rain.

INVESTIGATING THE EVIDENCE: TAIWAN, TYPHOONS AND EARTHQUAKES

The investigation: A team investigated Taiwan's typhoons to relate it to the occurrence of slow earthquakes.

The scientists: A team including Dr Selwyn Sacks and Dr Alan Linde of the Carnegie Institution, Department of Terrestrial Magnetism and Dr Chiching Liu of the Institute of Earth Sciences, Academia Sinica, Taiwan.

Collecting the evidence: Over a period of five years, from 2002 to 2007, the scientists measured changes in the rock and atmospheric variations over the Eurasian and the Philippine Sea Plates. The scientists used three highly sensitive borehole strainmeters 200–270m deep and 5–15km apart.

The conclusion: The team identified 20 slow earthquakes that lasted from several hours to more than a day. Of the 20, 11 slow earthquakes coincided with typhoons and were also stronger than the others. The scientists discovered that reduced atmospheric pressure caused by the typhoons releases the fault, causing a slow quake.

CHAPTER SEVEN

EARTHQUAKE PREDICTION

IT IS NOT POSSIBLE TO SAY EXACTLY WHEN A FUTURE EARTHQUAKE WILL HAPPEN, BUT ACCURATE EARTHQUAKE PREDICTIONS MAY BECOME A REALITY. IF OFFICIALS WERE TO ORDER PEOPLE TO LEAVE A CITY BECAUSE THEY BELIEVED AN EARTHQUAKE WAS COMING, BUT NOTHING HAPPENED, NOONE WOULD BELIEVE THE NEXT WARNING. SO, IT IS IMPORTANT THAT EARTHQUAKE PREDICTIONS ARE ACCURATE.

EARLY SUCCESS

When Chinese officials heard about strange movements of the land, changes in water levels and odd animal behaviour, they ordered people to leave the city of Haicheng. A few days later, on 4 February 1975, a strong earthquake hit the city. Thousands of lives were saved. Scientists wondered if earthquakes could be predicted by watching for these same warning signs. However, an even stronger earthquake struck the city of Tangshan the following year without any warning. Since then, scientists have developed more sensitive instruments, satellites and computer programs that can collect more information and analyze it in new ways. But they still have not been able to predict the exact place, time and strength of the next earthquake. The Northridge earthquake in California in 1994 and the Kobe earthquake in Japan in 1995 happened without warning.

MAKING FORECASTS

Some scientists are looking for patterns in small earthquakes that might hint at where and when the next big one will strike. If one day scientists could understand earthquake patterns in the same way as they understand weather patterns and forecasting, they may be able to predict when the next earthquake will happen.

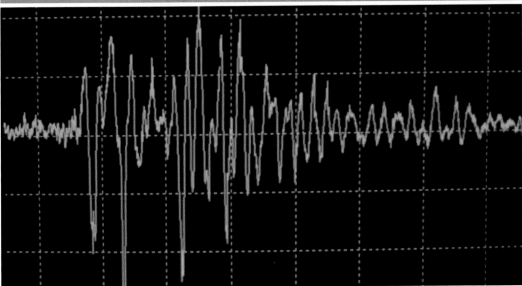

A man passes a leaning building amid destruction caused by the 1995 earthquake in Kobe, Japan (top). The seismograph (above) shows the strength of the earthquake which measured 7.1 on the Richter Scale.

Researchers clean up one of their search and rescue robots on its return from a training exercise.

ROBOT RESCUERS

Television pictures of a city just after an earthquake often show people digging through rubble with their bare hands to reach people buried underneath collapsed buildings. If trapped people can be located first, then the rescue workers know where to dig. Sensitive microphones lowered into the rubble can pick up sounds. Thermal cameras make pictures from heat instead of light. This means that the warmth of a human body shows up as a bright spot on the picture and it is easier to locate and rescue people. Tiny 'spy' cameras on the end of flexible cables can be fed inside small gaps in the rubble to see if there is anyone inside. And specially trained dogs can sniff out the scent of a buried person.

SEARCHING BY ROBOT

Today, most of the rescue work after an earthquake is done by hand, but in future robots may do much of the rescuing. The Center for Robot-Assisted Search and Rescue (CRASAR) at the University of South Florida in the USA has already developed a fleet of search and rescue robots which can be sent to help with rescue attempts after earthquakes.

▶ ▶ www.newscientist.com/article/dn17403-robot-rescue-rat-feels-its-way-through-rubble.html

This robot helps search and rescue personnel inspect disaster areas they cannot access.

Search and rescue robots are small so that they can get through tiny gaps in rubble. They have tracks like a tank to grip rough and uneven surfaces. They can be fitted with lights, cameras and equipment to help find people. The person steering the robot can see where it is going by looking at the pictures taken by the robot's cameras.

A NEW STANDARD

Search and rescue robots are already being tested. Robin Murphy from CRASAR has said that in five years when you see an earthquake on television, "You're going to see dogs and you're going to see robots. You're going to expect a rescue to have robots. It's going to be that standard."

A CAREER IN SCIENCE

Dr Robin Murphy is Raytheon Professor of Computer Science and Engineering at Texas A&M University, USA. Her basic research focuses on artificial intelligence and human-robot interaction for unmanned systems. She is a lead scientist in the field of rescue robots.

A DAY IN THE LIFE OF ...

Together with her colleagues, Dr Murphy develops robots to go into areas that would be dangerous for people. In 2003, the team developed a group of small robots that were sent in to search the ruins of an apartment building during an earthquake exercise in Indiana. The robots were equipped with thermal (heat) cameras and radar for finding trapped people. They successfully found someone inside the building. Robots have since been sent into other disaster areas.

THE SCIENTIST SAYS ...

"Through the Center for Robot-Assisted Search and Rescue, I have introduced ground, air, and sea robots to disaster response .... As fieldwork made it clear to me that the lack of understanding in the relationship between humans, robots and domains was the major stumbling block in diffusing these innovations to disaster management, my basic research turned to human-robot interaction."

EARTHQUAKE-PROOFING

Between 2000 and 2005, Mexico City experienced seven strong earthquakes. During that time, the tallest office building in Latin America was built in the city. It is called Torre Mayor. Engineers were certain that it would survive, because it was designed to withstand the strongest earthquakes. In places like Mexico City, where earthquakes are common, many new buildings are being designed to withstand strong shaking.

STABILIZING SKYSCRAPERS

Skyscrapers are made from concrete, steel and glass. They seem to be very stiff, but they can actually bend. They are designed to sway a little in strong winds and during earthquakes. But if they sway too far or too fast, they may start cracking. One way to protect a skyscraper is to brace it, or strengthen it, with extra beams to cut down on sideways shaking. Older,

smaller buildings can be strengthened in this way too. It is called retro-fitting. Skyscrapers can also be fitted with shock absorbers, or dampers. As the building bends or shakes, the dampers behave like cushions and soak up some of the energy. Torre Mayor has been fitted with nearly 100 of these dampers.

THE TOWER WITH THE SLIDING ROOF

The Applause Tower in Osaka, Japan, uses a different way of steadying itself during an earthquake. The flat top of the building is a helipad – a platform where helicopters land. The whole 480-tonne helipad

This 730-tonne mass damper hangs over four floors and equals out the movement of the Taipei 101 skyscraper in China during earthquakes and typhoons.

moves. If the building shakes too much during a quake, the helipad is automatically moved in the opposite direction to hold the building steady.

PROTECTING VULNERABLE BUILDINGS

Most people do not live in skyscrapers. About a third of the world's population live in houses, made from mud bricks, which collapse when an earthquake strikes. When the Iranian city of Bam suffered a strong earthquake in 2003, most of its mud brick buildings were destroyed. Scientists and engineers are trying to find ways to stop buildings like these from collapsing.

Torre Mayor in Mexico City is said to be the most earthquake-proof building in the world.

aftershock shaking of the ground that happens after a powerful earthquake

bedrock the solid rock that lies underneath the land

borehole a hole drilled into the ground – seismologists use boreholes to investigate ground movements in places where earthquakes are common

continental drift the movement of the great land masses across the Earth's surface, caused by plate tectonics

core the centre of the Earth, the solid inner core is surrounded by a liquid metal outer core

crust the topmost layer of the Earth, made from rock, it is about 30km thick where there are continents, and less than 10km thick under oceans

earthquake storm a series of large earthquakes that occur one after another, each quake triggering the next

earthquake swarm dozens, hundreds or thousands of small earthquakes occurring in the same place very quickly one after another

epicentre the point on the Earth's surface directly above the focus or hypocentre of an earthquake

fault a break or crack in the Earth's crust, where plates of rock meet, pull apart or grind against each other

focus the point under the ground where an earthquake originates, also called the hypocentre

foreshock shaking of the ground that happens before the most powerful shaking of an earthquake

geochemist a scientist who studies the chemistry of the Earth's rocks

geologist a scientist who studies the Earth's rocks and their history

geomorphologist a scientist who specializes in the study of landmass

geophysicist a scientist who studies the make-up of the Earth

geyser a hole in the ground where hot water and steam spurt out

Global Positioning System (GPS) a network of satellites that orbit the Earth and send the information they gather back down to the Earth

intensity the strength of shaking of the ground that is caused by an earthquake – intensity is measured on the Modified Mercali Intensity Scale

liquefaction an effect of some earthquakes that makes solid ground flow like a liquid

magma hot, molten (liquid) rock from the Earth's mantle

magnitude the strength of an earthquake,which is measured on the Richter Scale

mantle the layer of the Earth that lies between the core at the centre and the crust on the surface

marsquake shaking of the ground on the planet Mars

mega-quake a very powerful earthquake

Mercalli quake scale a means of recording the intensity of an earthquake by noting the amount of damage it causes

mid-ocean ridge a chain of mountains that stretches around the world under the oceans, where plates of rock are being pulled apart and molten rock comes up from below to form new ocean floor

moonquake shaking of the ground on the Moon

palaeoseismologist a scientist who studies ancient earthquakes, especially earthquakes that happened before recorded history

p waves the first and fastest of the energy waves produced by an earthquake

Richter Scale a way of describing the strength of an earthquake

seismic waves vibrations that travel outwards through the ground from the focus of an earthquake

seismograph a machine that produces a permanent record of an earthquake

seismologist a scientist who studies earthquakes

seismometer a machine that detects and measures an earthquake

shake table a model platform that can be vibrated to test the effect of an earthquake

subduction zone a place where one of the Earth's tectonic plates slides underneath another plate

surface waves the last energy waves produced by an earthquake, these are felt on the surface

s waves secondary vibrations produced by an earthquake, slower than p waves

tectonic plate one of the pieces that make up the Earth's crust

tremor a slight shaking of the ground. Foreshocks and aftershocks are examples of tremors

tsunami a giant wave, or series of waves, produced when part of the seabed is lifted suddenly by a quake